AF353161

Acknowledgments

This book is dedicated to my children
Arielle, **Daniel** and **Zekiel**.
May you continue to grow and flourish
as you explore the world around you.
Thank you for being my biggest inspiration.

To all the **Bajan Babies**, may you experience the joys
and culture of our beautiful Barbados,
throughout the years ahead.

To my husband **Garvin** and **my family**
and **dear friends**, thank you for your
continued prayers and support.

TO GOD BE THE GLORY!

Copyright © 2020 Terri-Ann Hopkin
Written by Terri-Ann Hopkin
Published by Cherry Tree Kids
cherrytreekids246@gmail.com

This book is sold subject to the condition that it shall not,
by way of trade or otherwise, be lent, scanned, photocopied,
resold, hired out or otherwise circulated without the publisher's prior
consent in any form of binding or cover other than that
in which it is published and without a similar condition including
this condition being imposed on the subsequent publisher.

ISBN: 978-81-945955-3-3

The moral right of the author has been asserted.

Illustrations Copyright © Terri-Ann Hopkin

Illustrations and Book Design by Uzuri Designs
www.uzuridesignsbooks.com
bookdesigner@uzuridesignsbooks.com

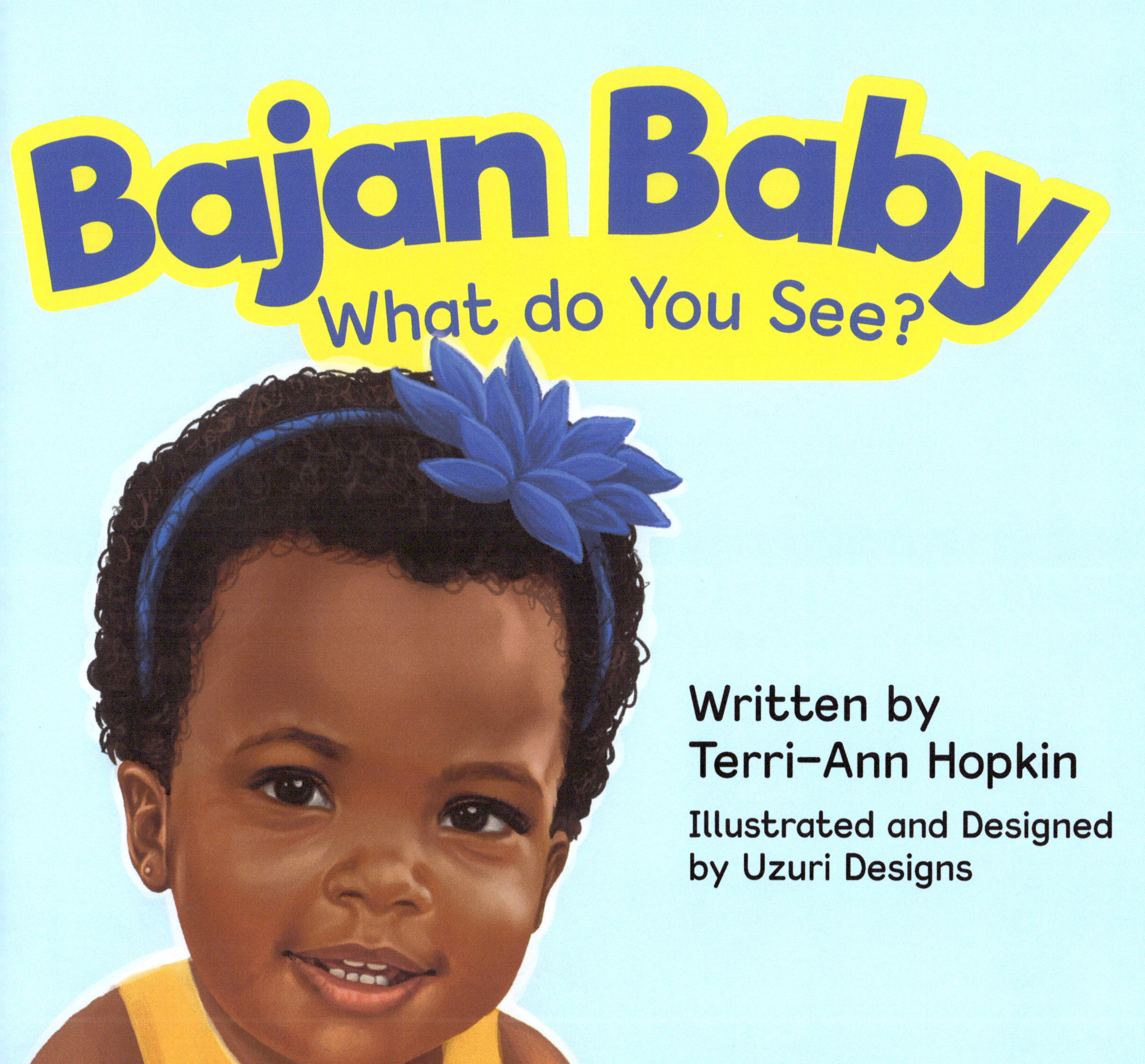

Bajan Baby
What do You See?

Written by
Terri-Ann Hopkin

Illustrated and Designed
by Uzuri Designs

Bajan Baby
what do you see?

I see a green monkey
looking at me.

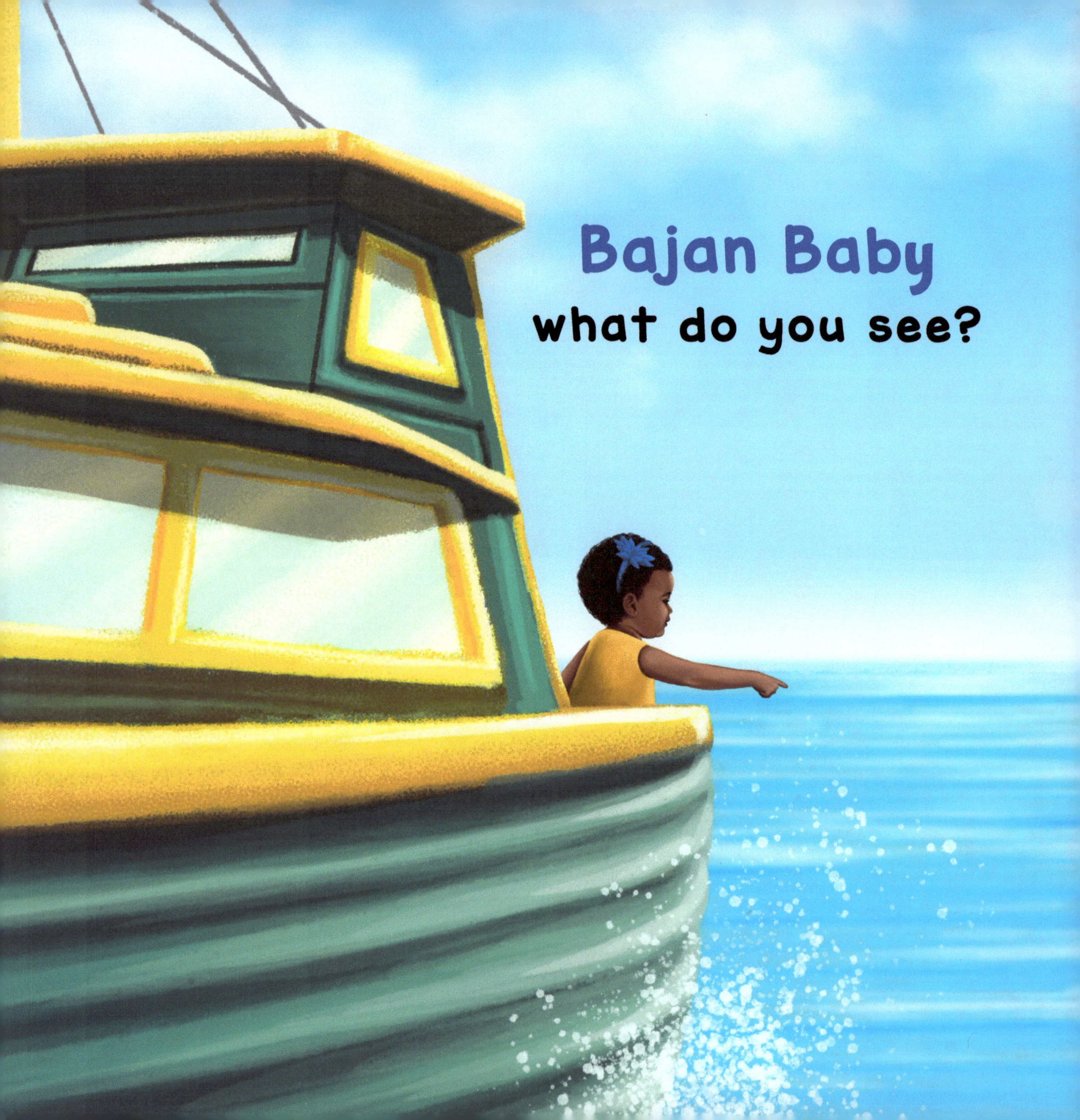

Bajan Baby
what do you see?

I see **flying fish** swimming in the sea.

Bajan Baby
what do you see?

I see school boys
eating ackees.

Bajan Baby what do you see?
I see black birds in a cherry tree.

Bajan Baby
what do you see?
Oistins Bay

I see
cou cou and flying fish!
Mmmm tasty!
arden

Bajan Baby
what do you see?

I see **beautiful caves** in St. Lucy.

Bajan Baby what do you see?
I see **Mother Sally** dancing merrily.

Bajan Baby
what do you see?

I see stiltmen walking as tall as can be.

Bajan Baby
what do you see?

I see the Tuk Band and landship
moving with glee.

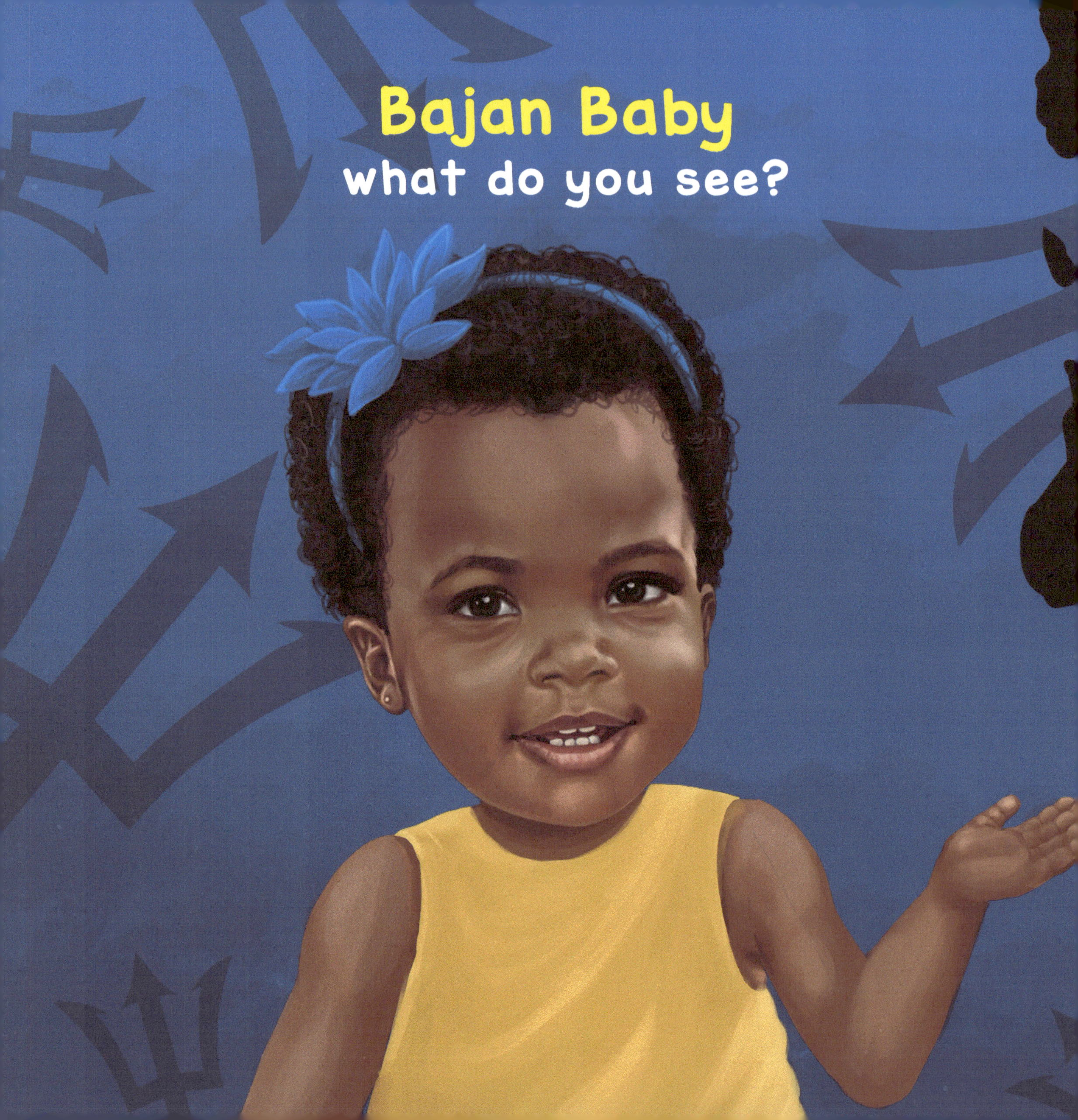

Bajan Baby
what do you see?

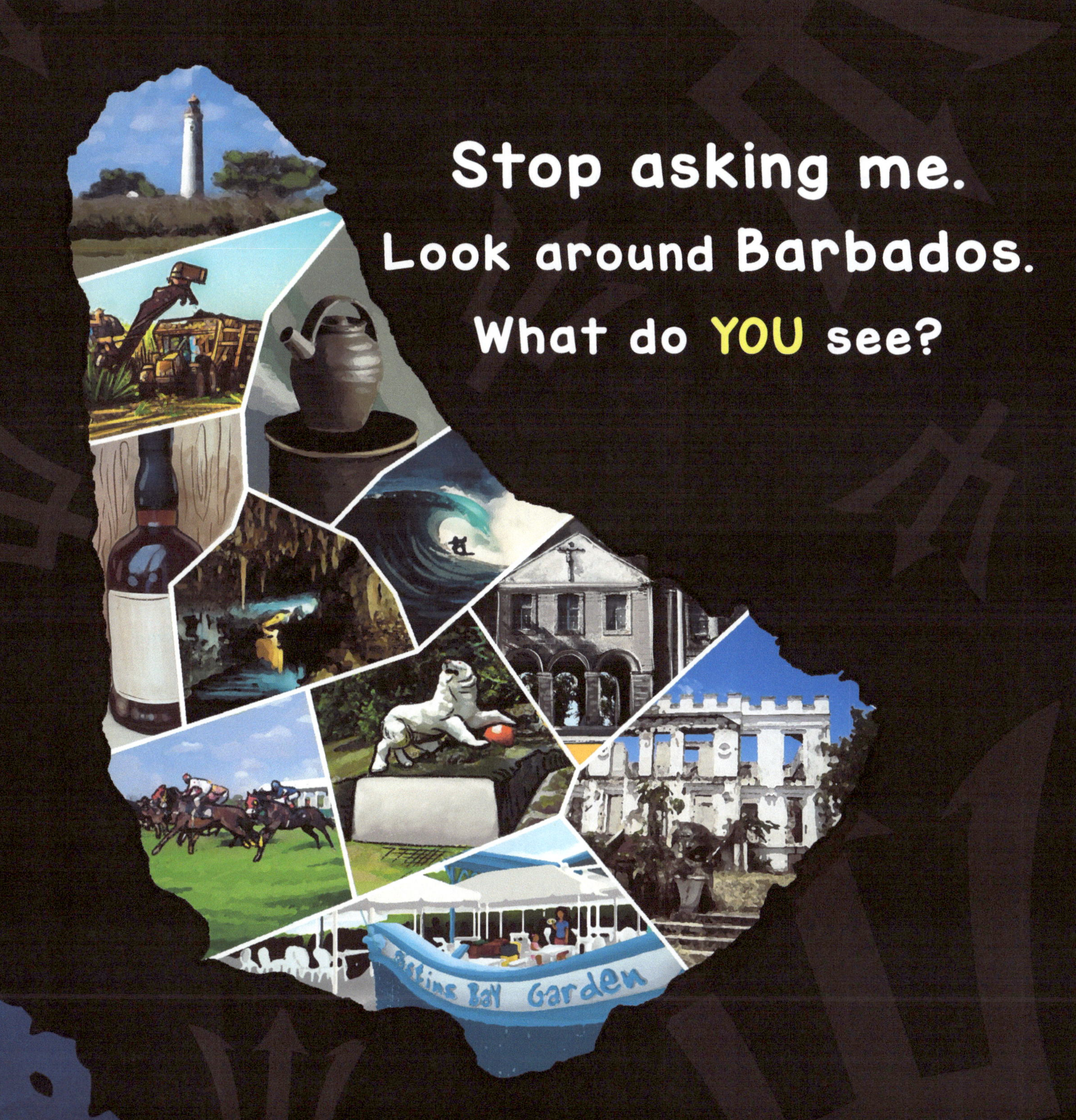

Stop asking me.
Look around Barbados.
What do YOU see?
Bathins Bay Garden

About the Author

Mrs. Terri-Ann Hopkin is a Trained Graduate Early Childhood Educator who has a passion for teaching young children. She gained certification in Early Childhood Education from the Servol Regional Training and Resource Centre, Trinidad and Tobago with a Credit, and then a Bachelors of Education in Early Childhood Care and Education from the University of the West Indies, St. Augustine with First Class Honours. Additionally she possesses a Diploma of Education (Primary), with a distinction. With over 17 years of experience in the field of Early Childhood Care and Education in Trinidad, Grenada and Barbados, and 5 plus years of parenthood, Terri-Ann has gained` an interest in children's literature and language and literacy development. It is through her experiences with her daughter that she was inspired to begin this journey as a children's author. Driven by passion and motivated by her three children along with the other children entrusted to her care, she is committed to providing young children with access to books that they can relate to; books that they can create authentic meaning from. **"Bajan Baby, What Do You See?"** is the first in a series of children's books inspired by children, for children in Barbados and the rest of the world.